Collins

Spelling

KS2 English Spelling

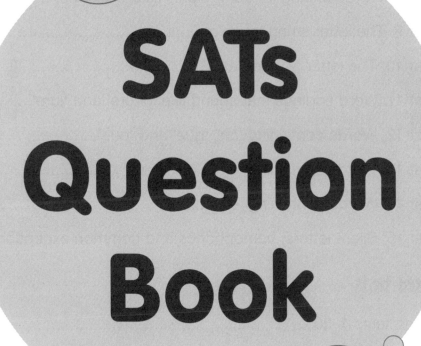

SATs Question Book

Age 10 – 11

Key Stage 2

SATs Question Book

 with audio

Shelley Welsh

Contents

Topic-based tests

Mixed tests

How to use this book

Use the spelling administration guide on page 1 of the pull-out booklet to read each spelling to your child. Allow them time to write it in the space provided.

 An audio version of the tests is available from our website:
www.collins.co.uk/collinsks2revision

Test 1: Words ending in -cious or -tious

Listen carefully to the missing word and fill in the answer space.

1 Mum's cakes are always _____.

1 mark

2 The archaeologist discovered a _____ jewel.

1 mark

3 On safari, we saw a _____ lion.

1 mark

4 My aunt has always been _____ about Friday 13th.

1 mark

5 Martha was _____ that she had not said thank you for her present.

1 mark

6 Chickenpox can be an _____ illness.

1 mark

7 We were a bit too _____ about how many miles we could walk.

1 mark

8 Our neighbour's dog can be quite _____.

1 mark

9 The Head Teacher has insisted pupils bring _____ packed lunches.

1 mark

10 I was very _____ as I walked down the cliff.

1 mark

Total marks .... /10   How am I doing?

Test 2: Words ending in -cial or -tial

Listen carefully to the missing word and fill in the answer space.

1 My favourite television _____ is the one for
chocolate!

2 When I saw our new puppy, my _____ reaction
was shock!

3 Our teacher said it was _____ that we listen to
her instructions.

4 After our tests, we are going on our Year 6 _____
for a week.

5 Whilst in Rome, they stayed in a _____ hotel.

6 Today in school, we learned about the _____
customs of the Incas.

7 Our Head Teacher said that our reports are _____.

8 My grandma prefers an _____ tree at Christmas.

9 Eleven o'clock is the _____ time to remember
those who lost their lives fighting for their country.

10 Eating fruit and vegetables is _____ to our health.

Total marks .... /10   How am I doing? 😊 😐 😣

Listen carefully to the missing word and fill in the answer space.

1 Our teaching _____ helps us with our times tables. <u>1 mark</u>

2 The younger children were creating a _____ in
the playground. <u>1 mark</u>

3 My brother was a _____ in a television quiz show. <u>1 mark</u>

4 Brogan's friend gave him some _____ on how to
use his new tablet. <u>1 mark</u>

5 The announcement of my auntie's _____ was
greeted with shouts of joy. <u>1 mark</u>

6 Zainab, who is very _____, soon noticed he'd
dropped his key. <u>1 mark</u>

7 We paid a _____ amount more for our new house. <u>1 mark</u>

8 Dad tried to book a hotel but there was no _____. <u>1 mark</u>

9 My sister needs a _____ aid in the swimming pool. <u>1 mark</u>

10 Uncle Arthur has been busy gardening since his _____
from the company. <u>1 mark</u>

Total marks .... /10   How am I doing? 😊 😐 ☹

Test 4: Words ending in -ent, -ence or -ency

Listen carefully to the missing word and fill in the answer space.

1 You can call an ambulance, the police or the fire brigade in

an _____.

1 mark

2 The whole school had to sit in _____ while we
waited for the Head Teacher.

1 mark

3 The bully didn't have the _____ to apologise,
even though she had done wrong.

1 mark

4 Gran's scarf was made from a _____, fine silk.

1 mark

5 The builders worked with great _____ and soon
finished.

1 mark

6 Katie's frequent _____ meant she had missed a
lot of work.

1 mark

7 Rebecca's _____ in French is due to many
holidays spent in Nice.

1 mark

8 The _____ of the mixture was thick and sticky.

1 mark

9 We decided the awful food was due to the _____
chef.

1 mark

10 Ben was in trouble for his _____ lack of attention.

1 mark

| Total marks .... /10 | How am I doing? ☺ 😐 ☹ |

6

Test 5: Words ending in -able, -ible, -ably or -ibly

Listen carefully to the missing word and fill in the answer space.

1 The cat was quite _____ lying on the windowsill.   1 mark

2 What a _____ day it is!   1 mark

3 It was _____ that our teacher was disappointed in our poor behaviour.   1 mark

4 Doing yoga has made my auntie very _____.   1 mark

5 It is _____ to drive more carefully in icy conditions.   1 mark

6 The policeman at the scene of the crime found there had been

a _____ entry.   1 mark

7 We have a _____ successful football team in our school.   1 mark

8 Our cousin behaved _____ when he crossed the road without looking.   1 mark

9 The band, which had entertained us all evening, _____ had to finish.   1 mark

10 There was a _____ big crack in the wall of our house.   1 mark

Total marks .... /10   How am I doing? ☺ 😐 ☹

Test 6: Adding suffixes to words ending in -fer

Listen carefully to the missing word and fill in the answer space.

1 My dad has a _____ for tomatoes rather than
cucumber in his salad.

1 mark

2 Mr Smith made a generous _____ to the animal
charity.

1 mark

3 The author _____ that the main character in the
book was lonely.

1 mark

4 Mum attended a _____ about healthy eating.

1 mark

5 The paintings were _____ to another gallery.

1 mark

6 My grandad has been _____ to a specialist doctor.

1 mark

7 The striker argued with the _____ when he didn't
spot the foul.

1 mark

8 I _____ the red dress to the blue one.

1 mark

9 My friend Grace is thinking of _____ to another
netball team.

1 mark

10 The judges _____ with each other when the two
teams drew.

1 mark

Total marks .... /10   How am I doing?

8

Listen carefully to the missing word and fill in the answer space.

1 Early in the morning, there is _____ on the inside of
our windows.

1 mark

2 There was an _____ spider in our bath this morning. 1 mark

3 My _____ little kitten scratched the armchair. 1 mark

4 When we heard the fire alarm, we went outside _____. 1 mark

5 The weather is _____ starting to improve. 1 mark

6 Our hotel _____ was outstanding. 1 mark

7 My dad _____ wants to climb Mount Everest. 1 mark

8 After banging his head, Dan was shaken but still _____. 1 mark

9 We showed our _____ by applauding the musicians. 1 mark

10 There won't _____ be extra break time just because
we are doing tests.

1 mark

Total marks .... /10   How am I doing?

9

Test 8: Words ending in -tion, -sion, -ssion or -cian

Listen carefully to the missing word and fill in the answer space.

1 There could only be one winner in the _____.

1 mark

2 The queen was relieved that the stolen jewel was back

in her _____.

1 mark

3 Our _____ was to have a picnic after our walk.

1 mark

4 The _____ pulled a rabbit out of his hat.

1 mark

5 Today in history, we learnt about the Roman _____.

1 mark

6 My brother mistakenly had the _____ that there
was no school today.

1 mark

7 Our teacher doesn't like it when there is an _____
during a lesson.

1 mark

8 There was an _____ fee of £5.00 for the school play.

1 mark

9 Mum likes to go to a _____ on special occasions.

1 mark

10 The wild dog showed his _____ when he was
captured.

1 mark

Total marks .... /10	How am I doing?	

Test 9: The letter string 'ough'

Listen carefully to the missing word and fill in the answer space.

1 Despite a _____ search, we were unable to find mum's ring.

1 mark

2 We didn't have _____ time to see all the sights in London.

1 mark

3 After a _____ start, Marcus took the lead and won the race.

1 mark

4 Freddy has had a bad _____ for a few days.

1 mark

5 The baker kneaded the _____ before placing it on a tray.

1 mark

6 We _____ our holiday to Wales was fantastic.

1 mark

7 Mia went sailing even _____ she gets seasick.

1 mark

8 I scratched my elbow on the _____ surface.

1 mark

9 When we got to the countryside, we saw farmers

_____ the fields.

1 mark

10 We really _____ to help our parents a bit more around the house.

1 mark

Total marks .... /10   How am I doing? ☺ 😐 ☹

Test 10: The letter 'y' used as 'i'

Listen carefully to the missing word and fill in the answer space.

1 My favourite stories are _____ and adventure.
1 mark

2 The multiplication _____ looks like the letter x.
1 mark

3 Dad's new _____ is blue and silver with ten gears.
1 mark

4 My uncle is a _____ teacher at the high school.
1 mark

5 The geologist discovered a rare _____ while on his field trip.
1 mark

6 We clapped out the _____ before we started singing the words.
1 mark

7 I am good at _____ because I am double-jointed.
1 mark

8 Mia and Joe had to play the _____ in the musical performance.
1 mark

9 Last week, we read the _____ about Perseus and the Kraken.
1 mark

10 My whole family enjoys any _____ exercise that keeps us healthy.
1 mark

Total marks .... /10   How am I doing?

12

Test 11: Word endings that sound like 'chure' and 'jure'

Listen carefully to the missing word and fill in the answer space.

1 We were asked to _____ the sides of the rectangle
then work out the area.

1 mark

2 The dog herded the sheep into their _____.

1 mark

3 Our grandad loves talking about his youthful _____.

1 mark

4 An aardvark, with its long snout, is quite an unusual

_____.

1 mark

5 The hills in the Lake District are a great place for a

_____ walk.

1 mark

6 It was with great _____ that our Head Teacher
accepted his retirement present.

1 mark

7 Mum confused us by moving the _____ around
yet again.

1 mark

8 The film was about an Egyptian mummy and some buried

_____.

1 mark

9 We painted _____ of our favourite animals.

1 mark

10 We had only a small amount of _____ time on our
class trip.

1 mark

Total marks .... /10   How am I doing? 😊 😐 🙁

Test 12: Words containing 'ch', 'gue' or 'que'

Listen carefully to the missing word and fill in the answer space.

1 My favourite _____ in the Harry Potter film is
Ron Weasley.

1 mark

2 When we went skiing, we stayed in a wooden _____. 1 mark

3 Mum asked for a _____ at the exhibition. 1 mark

4 When I went to the doctor with a sore throat, she asked me to stick my

_____ out. 1 mark

5 My mum has a _____ way of cooking spaghetti. 1 mark

6 We had to go to a _____ for plasters when my
brother cut his finger. 1 mark

7 Once we were down the ravine, we marvelled at the

_____ when we shouted out loud. 1 mark

8 Gran loves to watch TV programmes about _____. 1 mark

9 In the spring, I love being awakened to a _____
of birdsong. 1 mark

10 Our local restaurant has a wonderful new _____. 1 mark

Total marks .... /10   How am I doing?

14

Listen carefully to the missing word and fill in the answer space.

1 Blood is taken to the heart in _____ and taken
away in arteries.

1 mark

2 Our dog struggles to _____ us despite his many
training lessons.

1 mark

3 My _____ is very grumpy when we kick the ball
over her hedge.

1 mark

4 Mum let me _____ the flour when she was baking
the cake.

1 mark

5 The bride lifted her _____ so her new husband
could give her a kiss.

1 mark

6 We bought _____ new plants for our garden.

1 mark

7 The jockey pulled the _____ in when his horse bolted.

1 mark

8 My uncle _____ down the mountain for charity.

1 mark

9 The safari outfits were green, brown and _____ to
help camouflage the group.

1 mark

10 Our class did a _____ on how many pupils walked
to school.

1 mark

Total marks .... /10   How am I doing? ☺ 😐 😣

Test 14: Words containing 'ei'

Listen carefully to the missing word and fill in the answer space.

1 I _____ an award for being the top goal scorer this year.

1 mark

2 Dad painted the _____ with bright green paint.

1 mark

3 Make sure you keep the _____ in case you want to return the item you have bought.

1 mark

4 Too much _____ can keep you awake at night.

1 mark

5 Early last year, the explorer _____ the idea of a trek into the deepest jungles of Africa.

1 mark

6 It is important to include _____ in a healthy diet.

1 mark

7 The policewoman _____ the robber.

1 mark

8 The cheeky boy gave a _____ reply.

1 mark

9 It is important to get _____ currency before going abroad.

1 mark

10 The imposter tried to _____ the guard at the entrance.

1 mark

Total marks .... /10   How am I doing?

16

Test 15: Silent letters, homophones and common exceptions

Listen carefully to the missing word and fill in the answer space.

1 I carefully handed the _____ to my friend Harry.

_____
1 mark

2 The driver parked his _____ in the lay-by to allow the ambulance to get past.

_____
1 mark

3 The referee seemed to be _____ against the away team.

_____
1 mark

4 Many important decisions are made in _____.

_____
1 mark

5 The kitten was _____ by the candle flame.

_____
1 mark

6 When we went to the zoo, the pelicans appeared to

be _____.

_____
1 mark

7 Dad made a _____ when he sold his car.

_____
1 mark

8 Our teacher appeared very _____ so we knew someone was in trouble.

_____
1 mark

9 It was _____ that the snow would clear soon.

_____
1 mark

10 On the _____ night after Christmas, we took our tree down.

_____
1 mark

Total marks .... /10   How am I doing? 😊 😐 😣

Mixed Test 1

Listen carefully to the missing word and fill in the answer space.

1 The ballerina gave a _____ curtsey before leaving the stage.

1 mark

2 It is _____ to put your seat belt on when you are in the car.

1 mark

3 The tailor uses a high-tech sewing _____ to make expensive suits.

1 mark

4 My little sister is very _____ in the mornings.

1 mark

5 A _____ is an area of low pressure which produces rainy weather.

1 mark

6 We measured our _____ in maths today.

1 mark

7 Our new teacher is very _____ compared to our last one.

1 mark

8 Everyone was annoyed about the _____ of the swimming pool.

1 mark

9 In the first _____ of the play, the main actor forgot his words!

1 mark

10 I have an _____ watch but my brother's is digital.

1 mark

11 I _____ my friend Jake a present for his birthday.
_{1 mark}

12 Sam is a good _____ on me as he encourages me to work hard.
_{1 mark}

13 Getting stuck in traffic on the way to school is _____.
_{1 mark}

14 The Queen has had a long and successful _____.
_{1 mark}

15 My dad is always complaining about the _____ on the television.
_{1 mark}

16 The scar on my arm is now hardly _____.
_{1 mark}

17 When you know the name of the person you are writing to, you finish a

letter with 'Yours _____'.
_{1 mark}

18 Mum's favourite fish is _____.
_{1 mark}

19 We visited the _____ when we went to Egypt.
_{1 mark}

20 Matt's woollen coat was _____ in the wet weather.
_{1 mark}

Total marks .... /20　　　How am I doing?

19

Mixed Test 2

Listen carefully to the missing word and fill in the answer space.

1 We have two _____ lessons per week.

1 mark

2 My great-grandfather is _____ years old next year.

1 mark

3 The air traffic controller gave the pilot _____ to land.

1 mark

4 The explorers returned, suffering from _____ and thirst.

1 mark

5 Too much _____ to sun can be harmful to your skin.

1 mark

6 Erin displayed a lot of _____ on the obstacle course.

1 mark

7 My little sister is very _____ and believes everything I tell her!

1 mark

8 Joseph has been voted the best _____ in our year.

1 mark

9 I find it hard to _____ myself in the long summer holidays.

1 mark

10 Rome is a city full of _____ buildings.

1 mark

11 Mum likes to get a _____ when she goes shopping. 1 mark

12 Our teacher showed no _____ in my excuses about my late homework. 1 mark

13 My mum's _____ is French. 1 mark

14 There was a _____ smell coming from the restaurant kitchen. 1 mark

15 Twenty is _____ by two and ten. 1 mark

16 Dad wants us to move to a more _____ house. 1 mark

17 Five plus _____ equals five. 1 mark

18 Sometimes, wearing sunglasses can be a _____. 1 mark

19 The teacher decided we had tidied the art area

_____ well. 1 mark

20 The lion _____ attacked the gazelle. 1 mark

Total marks .... /20   How am I doing?

21

Mixed Test 3

Listen carefully to the missing word and fill in the answer space.

1 Joshua _____ his holiday photographs into school. 1 mark

2 It is not _____ to eat too much chocolate. 1 mark

3 We practise our _____ each day in English lessons. 1 mark

4 My older sister has left home and enjoys her _____. 1 mark

5 The naughty boy was _____ for his behaviour. 1 mark

6 Mum bought a _____ so that she could choose her new car. 1 mark

7 There was no _____ as to why our flower beds had been trampled in the night. 1 mark

8 We had to get _____ from our parents to go on the school trip. 1 mark

9 Dad's new car is _____ fast! 1 mark

10 We _____ go to Wales on holiday. 1 mark

22

11 My grandad is on a diet because he is _____.

1 mark

12 Most people in the twenty-first _____ own a mobile phone.

1 mark

13 To say that the hotel was first-class was an _____.

1 mark

14 Mr Shaw's _____ partner comes from Australia.

1 mark

15 The doctor gave Matt a prescription for some _____.

1 mark

16 The news that Billy had won the lottery turned out

to be _____.

1 mark

17 Our neighbour is an _____ golfer.

1 mark

18 There was a _____ between the train and the bus.

1 mark

19 Our teacher doesn't like it when she is _____.

1 mark

20 There was a _____ of ice-cream in the restaurant.

1 mark

Total marks .... /20   How am I doing?

Listen carefully to the missing word and fill in the answer space.

1 We are looking after my aunt's _____ puppy.   1 mark

2 It is _____ unlikely that the athlete will win a
gold medal.   1 mark

3 In our history lesson, we learnt about the soldiers who

_____ in World War II.   1 mark

4 Grandad's car had a _____ so he was late.   1 mark

5 I would like to _____ my congratulations to the
happy couple.   1 mark

6 After a while, the song sounded rather _____.   1 mark

7 We all agreed it was a _____ ending to an exciting
story.   1 mark

8 There was no _____ that the crime had been
committed by the man.   1 mark

9 After a _____ sunny day, we weren't too bothered
when the rain came.   1 mark

10 My dad says his _____ work really hard.   1 mark

11 After a _____ of wives, Henry VIII found one that he wanted to stay with.

1 mark

12 Our Head Teacher is going to retire _____.

1 mark

13 Stan's greatest _____ was winning the diving competition.

1 mark

14 In _____, Ahmed tried to attract the attention of the police car.

1 mark

15 The children had an _____ holiday in Scotland.

1 mark

16 My brother and I _____ the last piece of cake.

1 mark

17 Mum _____ goes to the market on Saturdays.

1 mark

18 Niamh was _____ the best choice for head girl.

1 mark

19 I had a _____ idea where the key had been left.

1 mark

20 We found the _____ locked in the safe.

1 mark

Total marks .... /20   How am I doing?

Mixed Test 5

Listen carefully to the missing word and fill in the answer space.

1 I like to _____ my new kitten's soft fur.

1 mark

2 Dad chose a stainless _____ oven for the new kitchen.

1 mark

3 The _____ started crying at the same time.

1 mark

4 Our school uniform is quite _____.

1 mark

5 The bullies were accused of spreading _____ gossip.

1 mark

6 The islanders use a _____ rope to make their fishing nets.

1 mark

7 The radio _____ was struggling with a very weak signal.

1 mark

8 We were told not to _____ our teacher on the school trip.

1 mark

9 My massive dog has the _____ to knock my frail grandad over.

1 mark

10 Whether it was warm or cold was _____ as the match had to go on.

1 mark

11 Stella has had _____ colds this winter.

1 mark

12 When using _____ in a story, you need to use inverted commas.

1 mark

13 It is _____ to be rude to adults.

1 mark

14 There is a lot of interesting _____ in Barcelona.

1 mark

15 We saw the _____ flash and heard the thunder roll.

1 mark

16 My little brother _____ threw his spaghetti on the floor.

1 mark

17 The flower emitted a beautiful _____.

1 mark

18 The _____ surrounded the Queen as she walked through the crowd.

1 mark

19 The boys _____ with each other in the playground.

1 mark

20 After a long day climbing, Joe was very _____.

1 mark

Total marks .... /20   How am I doing?

Mixed Test 6

Listen carefully to the missing word and fill in the answer space.

1 A _____ large play area has been requested by the local council.

2 Milo carried on running, _____ he knew he couldn't win.

3 Megan was _____ from the final race.

4 Our puppy _____ chewed Dad's slippers.

5 When you _____ twelve you get twenty-four.

6 The field is _____ from the country lane.

7 Our school trousers and skirts are _____ and our ties are red.

8 Mia baked the chocolate cream cake _____.

9 The teaching _____ can be very rewarding.

10 We watched our friend Mabel perform in the _____ competition.

11 In some _____, more than one god is worshipped. 1 mark

12 My _____ was sore after I ate too much ice-cream. 1 mark

13 Regular _____ can keep you fit and healthy. 1 mark

14 The weather was _____ awful the day we went to the seaside. 1 mark

15 My friend _____ Mum on her homemade cake. 1 mark

16 The view from the cliff top was _____. 1 mark

17 The smell of burning _____ as we got closer to the blaze. 1 mark

18 There was a _____ taste of ginger in the biscuit. 1 mark

19 We made a _____ search of the garden but still couldn't find the cat. 1 mark

20 A _____ is a speech made by one person. 1 mark

Total marks .... /20   How am I doing?

Mixed Test 7

Listen carefully to the missing word and fill in the answer space.

1 There was a _____ mess in the kitchen. 1 mark

2 Max crawled _____ the hedge to get the football. 1 mark

3 We knew we would be in _____ if we didn't get home soon. 1 mark

4 Our team is at the top of the _____. 1 mark

5 The zoo keepers _____ the escaped lion. 1 mark

6 We _____ hung up our wet coats before we sat by the fire. 1 mark

7 We like the _____ instruments in music lessons best of all. 1 mark

8 Mike's courage in rescuing the dog from the river

was _____. 1 mark

9 Our teacher _____ the sum. 1 mark

10 We had to _____ the circuit before we added the switch. 1 mark

Administration Guide

Read the following instruction out to your child.

I am going to read the sentences to you. Each sentence has a word missing. Listen carefully to the missing word and fill this in the answer space, making sure that you spell it correctly.

First I will read the word, then the word within a sentence, then repeat the word a third time.

You should now read the spellings three times, as given below. Leave at least a 12-second gap between spellings. At the end, read all the sentences again, giving your child the chance to make any changes they wish to their answers.

 An audio version of the tests is available from our website. www.collins.co.uk/collinsKS2revision

Test 1

1. The word is **delicious**. *Mum's cakes are always delicious*. The word is **delicious**.

2. The word is **precious**. *The archaeologist discovered a precious jewel*. The word is **precious**.

3. The word is **ferocious**. *On safari, we saw a ferocious lion*. The word is **ferocious**.

4. The word is **superstitious**. *My aunt has always been superstitious about Friday 13th*. The word is **superstitious**.

5. The word is **conscious**. *Martha was conscious that she had not said thank you for her present*. The word is **conscious**.

6. The word is **infectious**. *Chickenpox can be an infectious illness*. The word is **infectious**.

7. The word is **ambitious**. *We were a bit too ambitious about how many miles we could walk*. The word is **ambitious**.

8. The word is **vicious**. *Our neighbour's dog can be quite vicious*. The word is **vicious**.

9. The word is **nutritious**. *The Head Teacher has insisted pupils bring nutritious packed lunches*. The word is **nutritious**.

10. The word is **cautious**. *I was very cautious as I walked down the cliff*. The word is **cautious**.

Test 2

1. The word is **commercial**. *My favourite television commercial is the one for chocolate!* The word is **commercial**.

2. The word is **initial**. *When I saw our new puppy, my initial reaction was shock!* The word is **initial**.

3. The word is **crucial**. *Our teacher said it was crucial that we listen to her instructions*. The word is **crucial**.

4. The word is **residential**. *After our tests, we are going on our Year 6 residential for a week*. The word is **residential**.

5. The word is **palatial**. *Whilst in Rome, they stayed in a palatial hotel*. The word is **palatial**.

6. The word is **sacrificial**. *Today in school, we learned about the sacrificial customs of the Incas*. The word is **sacrificial**.

7. The word is **confidential**. *Our Head Teacher said that our reports are confidential*. The word is **confidential**.

8. The word is **artificial**. *My grandma prefers an artificial tree at Christmas*. The word is **artificial**.

9. The word is **official**. *Eleven o'clock is the official time to remember those who lost their lives fighting for their country*. The word is **official**.

10. The word is **beneficial**. *Eating fruit and vegetables is beneficial to our health*. The word is **beneficial**.

Test 3

1. The word is **assistant**. *Our teaching assistant helps us with our times tables*. The word is **assistant**.

2. The word is **disturbance**. *The younger children were creating a disturbance in the playground*. The word is **disturbance**.

3. The word is **participant**. *My brother was a participant in a television quiz show*. The word is **participant**.

4. The word is **guidance**. *Brogan's friend gave him some guidance on how to use his new tablet*. The word is **guidance**.

5. The word is **pregnancy**. *The announcement of my auntie's pregnancy was greeted with shouts of joy*. The word is **pregnancy**.

6. The word is **observant**. *Zainab, who is very observant, soon noticed he'd dropped his key*. The word is **observant**.

7. The word is **significant**. *We paid a significant amount more for our new house*. The word is **significant**.

8. The word is **vacancy**. *Dad tried to book a hotel but there was no vacancy*. The word is **vacancy**.

9. The word is **buoyancy**. *My sister needs a buoyancy aid in the swimming pool*. The word is **buoyancy**.

10. The word is **redundancy**. *Uncle Arthur has been busy gardening since his redundancy from the company*. The word is **redundancy**.

Test 4

1. The word is **emergency**. *You can call an ambulance, the police or the fire brigade in an emergency*. The word is **emergency**.

2. The word is **silence**. *The whole school had to sit in silence while we waited for the Head Teacher*. The word is **silence**.

3. The word is **decency**. *The bully didn't have the decency to apologise, even though she had done wrong*. The word is **decency**.

4. The word is **transparent**. *Gran's scarf was made from a transparent, fine silk*. The word is **transparent**.

5. The word is **efficiency**. *The builders worked with great efficiency and soon finished*. The word is **efficiency**.

6. The word is **absence**. *Katie's frequent absence meant she had missed a lot of work.* The word is **absence**.

7. The word is **fluency**. *Rebecca's fluency in French is due to many holidays spent in Nice.* The word is **fluency**.

8. The word is **consistency**. *The consistency of the mixture was thick and sticky.* The word is **consistency**.

9. The word is **incompetent**. *We decided the awful food was due to the incompetent chef.* The word is **incompetent**.

10. The word is **consistent**. *Ben was in trouble for his consistent lack of attention.* The word is **consistent**.

Test 5

1. The word is **comfortable**. *The cat was quite comfortable lying on the windowsill.* The word is **comfortable**.

2. The word is **horrible**. *What a horrible day it is!* The word is **horrible**.

3. The word is **understandable**. *It was understandable that our teacher was disappointed in our poor behaviour.* The word is **understandable**.

4. The word is **flexible**. *Doing yoga has made my auntie very flexible.* The word is **flexible**.

5. The word is **advisable**. *It is advisable to drive more carefully in icy conditions.* The word is **advisable**.

6. The word is **forcible**. *The policeman at the scene of the crime found there had been a forcible entry.* The word is **forcible**.

7. The word is **remarkably**. *We have a remarkably successful football team in our school.* The word is **remarkably**.

8. The word is **irresponsibly**. *Our cousin behaved irresponsibly when he crossed the road without looking.* The word is **irresponsibly**.

9. The word is **regrettably**. *The band, which had entertained us all evening, regrettably had to finish.* The word is **regrettably**.

10. The word is **noticeably**. *There was a noticeably big crack in the wall of our house.* The word is **noticeably**.

Test 6

1. The word is **preference**. *My dad has a preference for tomatoes rather than cucumber in his salad.* The word is **preference**.

2. The word is **offering**. *Mr Smith made a generous offering to the animal charity.* The word is **offering**.

3. The word is **inferred**. *The author inferred that the main character in the book was lonely.* The word is **inferred**.

4. The word is **conference**. *Mum attended a conference about healthy eating.* The word is **conference**.

5. The word is **transferred**. *The paintings were transferred to another gallery.* The word is **transferred**.

6. The word is **referred**. *My grandad has been referred to a specialist doctor.* The word is **referred**.

7. The word is **referee**. *The striker argued with the referee when he didn't spot the foul.* The word is **referee**.

8. The word is **preferred**. *I preferred the red dress to the blue one.* The word is **preferred**.

9. The word is **transferring**. *My friend Grace is thinking of transferring to another netball team.* The word is **transferring**.

10. The word is **conferred**. *The judges conferred with each other when the two teams drew.* The word is **conferred**.

Test 7

1. The word is **condensation**. *Early in the morning, there is condensation on the inside of our windows.* The word is **condensation**.

2. The word is **enormous**. *There was an enormous spider in our bath this morning.* The word is **enormous**.

3. The word is **mischievous**. *My mischievous little kitten scratched the armchair.* The word is **mischievous**.

4. The word is **immediately**. *When we heard the fire alarm, we went outside immediately.* The word is **immediately**.

5. The word is **definitely**. *The weather is definitely starting to improve.* The word is **definitely**.

6. The word is **accommodation**. *Our hotel accommodation was outstanding.* The word is **accommodation**.

7. The word is **desperately**. *My dad desperately wants to climb Mount Everest.* The word is **desperately**.

8. The word is **conscious**. *After banging his head, Dan was shaken but still conscious.* The word is **conscious**.

9. The word is **appreciation**. *We showed our appreciation by applauding the musicians.* The word is **appreciation**.

10. The word is **necessarily**. *There won't necessarily be extra break time just because we are doing tests.* The word is **necessarily**.

Test 8

1. The word is **competition**. *There could only be one winner in the competition.* The word is **competition**.

2. The word is **possession**. *The queen was relieved that the stolen jewel was back in her possession.* The word is **possession**.

3. The word is **intention**. *Our intention was to have a picnic after our walk.* The word is **intention**.

4. The word is **magician**. *The magician pulled a rabbit out of his hat.* The word is **magician**.

5. The word is **invasion**. *Today in history, we learnt about the Roman invasion.* The word is **invasion**.

6. The word is **impression**. *My brother mistakenly had the impression that there was no school today.* The word is **impression**.

7. The word is **interruption**. *Our teacher doesn't like it when there is an interruption during a lesson.* The word is **interruption**.

8. The word is **admission**. *There was an admission fee of £5.00 for the school play.* The word is **admission**.

9. The word is **beautician**. *Mum likes to go to a beautician on special occasions.* The word is **beautician**.

10. The word is **aggression**. *The wild dog showed his aggression when he was captured.* The word is **aggression**.

Test 9

1. The word is **thorough**. *Despite a thorough search, we were unable to find mum's ring.* The word is **thorough**.

2. The word is **enough**. *We didn't have enough time to see all the sights in London.* The word is **enough**.

3. The word is **tough**. *After a tough start, Marcus took the lead and won the race.* The word is **tough**.

4. The word is **cough**. *Freddy has had a bad cough for a few days.* The word is **cough**.

5. The word is **dough**. The baker kneaded the **dough** before placing it on a tray. The word is **dough**.

6. The word is **thought**. *We thought our holiday to Wales was fantastic.* The word is **thought**.

7. The word is **though**. *Mia went sailing even though she gets seasick.* The word is **though**.

8. The word is **rough**. *I scratched my elbow on the rough surface.* The word is **rough**.

9. The word is **ploughing**. *When we got to the countryside, we saw farmers ploughing the fields.* The word is **ploughing**.

10. The word is **ought**. *We really ought to help our parents a bit more around the house.* The word is **ought**.

Test 10

1. The word is **mystery**. *My favourite stories are mystery and adventure.* The word is **mystery**.

2. The word is **symbol**. *The multiplication symbol looks like the letter x.* The word is **symbol**.

3. The word is **bicycle**. *Dad's new bicycle is blue and silver with ten gears.* The word is **bicycle**.

4. The word is **physics**. *My uncle is a physics teacher at the high school.* The word is **physics**.

5. The word is **crystal**. *The geologist discovered a rare crystal while on his field trip.* The word is **crystal**.

6. The word is **rhythm**. *We clapped out the rhythm before we started singing the words.* The word is **rhythm**.

7. The word is **gymnastics**. *I am good at gymnastics because I am double-jointed.* The word is **gymnastics**.

8. The word is **cymbals**. *Mia and Joe had to play the cymbals in the musical performance.* The word is **cymbals**.

9. The word is **myth**. *Last week, we read the myth about Perseus and the Kraken.* The word is **myth**.

10. The word is **physical**. *My whole family enjoys any physical exercise that keeps us healthy.* The word is **physical**.

Test 11

1. The word is **measure**. *We were asked to measure the sides of the rectangle then work out the area.* The word is **measure**.

2. The word is **enclosure**. *The dog herded the sheep into their enclosure.* The word is **enclosure**.

3. The word is **adventures**. *Our grandad loves talking about his youthful adventures.* The word is **adventures**.

4. The word is **creature**. *An aardvark, with its long snout, is quite an unusual creature.* The word is **creature**.

5. The word is **nature**. *The hills in the Lake District are a great place for a nature walk.* The word is **nature**.

6. The word is **pleasure**. *It was with great pleasure that our Head Teacher accepted his retirement present.* The word is **pleasure**.

7. The word is **furniture**. *Mum confused us by moving the furniture around yet again.* The word is **furniture**.

8. The word is **treasure**. *The film was about an Egyptian mummy and some buried treasure.* The word is **treasure**.

9. The word is **pictures**. *We painted pictures of our favourite animals.* The word is **pictures**.

10. The word is **leisure**. *We had only a small amount of leisure time on our class trip.* The word is **leisure**.

Test 12

1. The word is **character**. *My favourite character in the Harry Potter film is Ron Weasley.* The word is **character**.

2. The word is **chalet**. *When we went skiing, we stayed in a wooden chalet.* The word is **chalet**.

3. The word is **brochure**. *Mum asked for a brochure at the exhibition.* The word is **brochure**.

4. The word is **tongue**. *When I went to the doctor with a sore throat, she asked me to stick my tongue out.* The word is **tongue**.

5. The word is **unique**. *My mum has a unique way of cooking spaghetti.* The word is **unique**.

6. The word is **chemist**. *We had to go to a chemist for plasters when my brother cut his finger.* The word is **chemist**.

7. The word is **echo**. *Once we were down the ravine, we marvelled at the echo when we shouted out loud.* The word is **echo**.

8. The word is **antiques**. *Gran loves to watch TV programmes about antiques.* The word is **antiques**.

9. The word is **chorus**. *In the spring, I love being awakened to a chorus of birdsong.* The word is **chorus**.

10. The word is **chef**. *Our local restaurant has a wonderful new chef.* The word is **chef**.

Test 13

1. The word is **veins**. *Blood is taken to the heart in veins and taken away in arteries.* The word is **veins**.

2. The word is **obey**. *Our dog struggles to obey us despite his many training lessons.* The word is **obey**.

3. The word is **neighbour**. *My neighbour is very grumpy when we kick the ball over her hedge.* The word is **neighbour**.

4. The word is **weigh**. *Mum let me weigh the flour when she was baking the cake.* The word is **weigh**.

5. The word is **veil**. *The bride lifted her veil so her new husband could give her a kiss.* The word is **veil**.

6. The word is **eight**. *We bought eight new plants for our garden.* The word is **eight**.

7. The word is **reins**. *The jockey pulled the reins in when his horse bolted.* The word is **reins**.

8. The word is **abseiled**. *My uncle abseiled down the mountain for charity.* The word is **abseiled**.

9. The word is **beige**. *The safari outfits were green, brown and beige to help camouflage the group.* The word is **beige**.

10. The word is **survey**. *Our class did a survey on how many pupils walked to school.* The word is **survey**.

Test 14

1. The word is **received**. *I received an award for being the top goal scorer this year.* The word is **received**.

2. The word is **ceiling**. *Dad painted the ceiling with bright green paint.* The word is **ceiling**.

3. The word is **receipt**. *Make sure you keep the receipt in case you want to return the item you have bought.* The word is **receipt**.

4. The word is **caffeine**. *Too much caffeine can keep you awake at night.* The word is **caffeine**.

5. The word is **conceived**. *Early last year, the explorer conceived the idea of a trek into the deepest jungles of Africa.* The word is **conceived**.

6. The word is **protein**. *It is important to include **protein** in a healthy diet. The word is **protein**.*

7. The word is **seized**. *The policewoman **seized** the robber. The word is **seized**.*

8. The word is **conceited**. *The cheeky boy gave a **conceited** reply. The word is **conceited**.*

9. The word is **foreign**. *It is important to get **foreign** currency before going abroad. The word is **foreign**.*

10. The word is **deceive**. *The imposter tried to **deceive** the guard at the entrance. The word is **deceive**.*

Test 15

1. The word is **scissors**. *I carefully handed the **scissors** to my friend Harry. The word is **scissors**.*

2. The word is **vehicle**. *The driver parked his **vehicle** in the lay-by to allow the ambulance to get past. The word is **vehicle**.*

3. The word is **prejudiced**. *The referee seemed to be **prejudiced** against the away team. The word is **prejudiced**.*

4. The word is **parliament**. *Many important decisions are made in **parliament**. The word is **parliament**.*

5. The word is **fascinated**. *The kitten was **fascinated** by the candle flame. The word is **fascinated**.*

6. The word is **stationary**. *When we went to the zoo, the pelicans appeared to be **stationary**. The word is **stationary**.*

7. The word is **profit**. *Dad made a **profit** when he sold his car. The word is **profit**.*

8. The word is **solemn**. *Our teacher appeared very **solemn** so we knew someone was in trouble. The word is **solemn**.*

9. The word is **doubtful**. *It was **doubtful** that the snow would clear soon. The word is **doubtful**.*

10. The word is **twelfth**. *On the **twelfth** night after Christmas, we took our tree down. The word is **twelfth**.*

Mixed Test 1

1. The word is **gracious**. *The ballerina gave a **gracious** curtsey before leaving the stage. The word is **gracious**.*

2. The word is **important**. *It is **important** to put your seat belt on when you are in the car. The word is **important**.*

3. The word is **machine**. *The tailor uses a high-tech sewing **machine** to make expensive suits. The word is **machine**.*

4. The word is **irritable**. *My little sister is very **irritable** in the mornings. The word is **irritable**.*

5. The word is **depression**. *A **depression** is an area of low pressure which produces rainy weather. The word is **depression**.*

6. The word is **height**. *We measured our **height** in maths today. The word is **height**.*

7. The word is **dynamic**. *Our new teacher is very **dynamic** compared to our last one. The word is **dynamic**.*

8. The word is **closure**. *Everyone was annoyed about the **closure** of the swimming pool. The word is **closure**.*

9. The word is **scene**. *In the first **scene** of the play, the main actor forgot his words! The word is **scene**.*

10. The word is **analogue**. *I have an **analogue** watch but my brother's is digital. The word is **analogue**.*

11. The word is **bought**. *I **bought** my friend Jake a present for his birthday. The word is **bought**.*

12. The word is **influence**. *Sam is a good **influence** on me as he encourages me to work hard. The word is **influence**.*

13. The word is **unavoidable**. *Getting stuck in traffic on the way to school is **unavoidable**. The word is **unavoidable**.*

14. The word is **reign**. *The Queen has had a long and successful **reign**. The word is **reign**.*

15. The word is **politicians**. *My dad is always complaining about the **politicians** on the television. The word is **politicians**.*

16. The word is **noticeable**. *The scar on my arm is now hardly **noticeable**. The word is **noticeable**.*

17. The word is **sincerely**. *When you know the name of the person you are writing to, you finish a letter with 'Yours **sincerely**'. The word is **sincerely**.*

18. The word is **salmon**. *Mum's favourite fish is **salmon**. The word is **salmon**.*

19. The word is **pyramids**. *We visited the **pyramids** when we went to Egypt. The word is **pyramids**.*

20. The word is **impractical**. *Matt's woollen coat was **impractical** in the wet weather. The word is **impractical**.*

Mixed Test 2

1. The word is **science**. *We have two **science** lessons per week. The word is **science**.*

2. The word is **eighty**. *My great-grandfather is **eighty** years old next year. The word is **eighty**.*

3. The word is **clearance**. *The air traffic controller gave the pilot **clearance** to land. The word is **clearance**.*

4. The word is **fatigue**. *The explorers returned, suffering from **fatigue** and thirst. The word is **fatigue**.*

5. The word is **exposure**. *Too much **exposure** to sun can be harmful to your skin. The word is **exposure**.*

6. The word is **confidence**. *Erin displayed a lot of **confidence** on the obstacle course. The word is **confidence**.*

7. The word is **gullible**. *My little sister is very **gullible** and believes everything I tell her! The word is **gullible**.*

8. The word is **musician**. *Joseph has been voted the best **musician** in our year. The word is **musician**.*

9. The word is **occupy**. *I find it hard to **occupy** myself in the long summer holidays. The word is **occupy**.*

10. The word is **historical**. *Rome is a city full of **historical** buildings. The word is **historical**.*

11. The word is **bargain**. *Mum likes to get a **bargain** when she goes shopping. The word is **bargain**.*

12. The word is **interest**. *Our teacher showed no **interest** in my excuses about my late homework. The word is **interest**.*

13. The word is **nationality**. *My mum's **nationality** is French. The word is **nationality**.*

14. The word is **peculiar**. *There was a **peculiar** smell coming from the restaurant kitchen. The word is **peculiar**.*

15. The word is **divisible**. *Twenty is **divisible** by two and ten. The word is **divisible**.*

16. The word is **spacious**. *Dad wants us to move to a more **spacious** house. The word is **spacious**.*

17. The word is **nought**. *Five plus nought equals five.* The word is **nought**.

18. The word is **hindrance**. *Sometimes, wearing sunglasses can be a hindrance.* The word is **hindrance**.

19. The word is **sufficiently**. *The teacher decided we had tidied the art area sufficiently well.* The word is **sufficiently**.

20. The word is **ferociously**. *The lion ferociously attacked the gazelle.* The word is **ferociously**.

Mixed Test 3

1. The word is **brought**. *Joshua brought his holiday photographs into school.* The word is **brought**.

2. The word is **sensible**. *It is not sensible to eat too much chocolate.* The word is **sensible**.

3. The word is **grammar**. *We practise our grammar each day in English lessons.* The word is **grammar**.

4. The word is **independence**. *My older sister has left home and enjoys her independence.* The word is **independence**.

5. The word is **disciplined**. *The naughty boy was disciplined for his behaviour.* The word is **disciplined**.

6. The word is **catalogue**. *Mum bought a catalogue so that she could choose her new car.* The word is **catalogue**.

7. The word is **explanation**. *There was no explanation as to why our flower beds had been trampled in the night.* The word is **explanation**.

8. The word is **permission**. *We had to get permission from our parents to go on the school trip.* The word is **permission**.

9. The word is **unbelievably**. *Dad's new car is unbelievably fast!* The word is **unbelievably**.

10. The word is **frequently**. *We frequently go to Wales on holiday.* The word is **frequently**.

11. The word is **overweight**. *My grandad is on a diet because he is overweight.* The word is **overweight**.

12. The word is **century**. *Most people in the twenty-first century own a mobile phone.* The word is **century**.

13. The word is **exaggeration**. *To say that the hotel was first-class was an exaggeration.* The word is **exaggeration**.

14. The word is **business**. *Mr Shaw's business partner comes from Australia.* The word is **business**.

15. The word is **medicine**. *The doctor gave Matt a prescription for some medicine.* The word is **medicine**.

16. The word is **fictitious**. *The news that Billy had won the lottery turned out to be fictitious.* The word is **fictitious**.

17. The word is **amateur**. *Our neighbour is an amateur golfer.* The word is **amateur**.

18. The word is **collision**. *There was a collision between the train and the bus.* The word is **collision**.

19. The word is **interrupted**. *Our teacher doesn't like it when she is interrupted.* The word is **interrupted**.

20. The word is **variety**. *There was a variety of ice-cream in the restaurant.* The word is **variety**.

Mixed Test 4

1. The word is **young**. *We are looking after my aunt's young puppy.* The word is **young**.

2. The word is **incredibly**. *It is incredibly unlikely that the athlete will win a gold medal.* The word is **incredibly**.

3. The word is **fought**. *In our history lesson, we learnt about the soldiers who fought in World War II.* The word is **fought**.

4. The word is **puncture**. *Grandad's car had a puncture so he was late.* The word is **puncture**.

5. The word is **convey**. *I would like to convey my congratulations to the happy couple.* The word is **convey**.

6. The word is **repetitious**. *After a while, the song sounded rather repetitious.* The word is **repetitious**.

7. The word is **marvellous**. *We all agreed it was a marvellous ending to an exciting story.* The word is **marvellous**.

8. The word is **evidence**. *There was no evidence that the crime had been committed by the man.* The word is **evidence**.

9. The word is **reasonably**. *After a reasonably sunny day, we weren't too bothered when the rain came.* The word is **reasonably**.

10. The word is **colleagues**. *My dad says his colleagues work really hard.* The word is **colleagues**.

11. The word is **succession**. *After a succession of wives, Henry VIII found one that he wanted to stay with.* The word is **succession**.

12. The word is **apparently**. *Our Head Teacher is going to retire apparently.* The word is **apparently**.

13. The word is **achievement**. *Stan's greatest achievement was winning the diving competition.* The word is **achievement**.

14. The word is **desperation**. *In desperation, Ahmed tried to attract the attention of the police car.* The word is **desperation**.

15. The word is **adventurous**. *The children had an adventurous holiday in Scotland.* The word is **adventurous**.

16. The word is **halved**. *My brother and I halved the last piece of cake.* The word is **halved**.

17. The word is **regularly**. *Mum regularly goes to the market on Saturdays.* The word is **regularly**.

18. The word is **unquestionably**. *Niamh was unquestionably the best choice for head girl.* The word is **unquestionably**.

19. The word is **vague**. *I had a vague idea where the key had been left.* The word is **vague**.

20. The word is **jewellery**. *We found the jewellery locked in the safe.* The word is **jewellery**.

Mixed Test 5

1. The word is **touch**. *I like to touch my new kitten's soft fur.* The word is **touch**.

2. The word is **steel**. *Dad chose a stainless steel oven for the new kitchen.* The word is **steel**.

3. The word is **babies**. *The babies started crying at the same time.* The word is **babies**.

4. The word is **fashionable**. *Our school uniform is quite fashionable.* The word is **fashionable**.

5. The word is **malicious**. *The bullies were accused of spreading malicious gossip.* The word is **malicious**.

6. The word is **tough**. *The islanders use a tough rope to make their fishing nets.* The word is **tough**.

7. The word is **transmission**. *The radio transmission was struggling with a very weak signal.* The word is **transmission**.

8. The word is **disobey**. *We were told not to disobey our teacher on the school trip.* The word is **disobey**.

9. The word is **potential**. *My massive dog has the potential to knock my frail grandad over.* The word is **potential**.

10. The word is **irrelevant**. *Whether it was warm or cold was irrelevant as the match had to go on.* The word is **irrelevant**.

11. The word is **frequent**. *Stella has had frequent colds this winter.* The word is **frequent**.

12. The word is **dialogue**. *When using dialogue in a story, you need to use inverted commas.* The word is **dialogue**.

13. The word is **unacceptable**. *It is unacceptable to be rude to adults.* The word is **unacceptable**.

14. The word is **architecture**. *There is a lot of interesting architecture in Barcelona.* The word is **architecture**.

15. The word is **lightning**. *We saw the lightning flash and heard the thunder roll.* The word is **lightning**.

16. The word is **naughtily**. *My little brother naughtily threw his spaghetti on the floor.* The word is **naughtily**.

17. The word is **fragrance**. *The flower emitted a beautiful fragrance.* The word is **fragrance**.

18. The word is **guards**. *The guards surrounded the Queen as she walked through the crowd.* The word is **guards**.

19. The word is **wrestled**. *The boys wrestled with each other in the playground.* The word is **wrestled**.

20. The word is **weary**. *After a long day climbing, Joe was very weary.* The word is **weary**.

Mixed Test 6

1. The word is **suitably**. *A suitably large play area has been requested by the local council.* The word is **suitably**.

2. The word is **although**. *Milo carried on running, although he knew he couldn't win.* The word is **although**.

3. The word is **disqualified**. *Megan was disqualified from the final race.* The word is **disqualified**.

4. The word is **mischievously**. *Our puppy mischievously chewed Dad's slippers.* The word is **mischievously**.

5. The word is **double**. *When you double twelve you get twenty-four.* The word is **double**.

6. The word is **accessible**. *The field is accessible from the country lane.* The word is **accessible**.

7. The word is **grey**. *Our school trousers and skirts are grey and our ties are red.* The word is **grey**.

8. The word is **expertly**. *Mia baked the chocolate cream cake expertly.* The word is **expertly**.

9. The word is **profession**. *The teaching profession can be very rewarding.* The word is **profession**.

10. The word is **gymnastics**. *We watched our friend Mabel perform in the gymnastics competition.* The word is **gymnastics**.

11. The word is **cultures**. *In some cultures, more than one god is worshipped.* The word is **cultures**.

12. The word is **stomach**. *My stomach was sore after I ate too much ice-cream.* The word is **stomach**.

13. The word is **exercise**. *Regular exercise can keep you fit and healthy.* The word is **exercise**.

14. The word is **indescribably**. *The weather was indescribably awful the day we went to the seaside.* The word is **indescribably**.

15. The word is **complimented**. *My friend complimented Mum on her homemade cake.* The word is **complimented**.

16. The word is **spectacular**. *The view from the cliff top was spectacular.* The word is **spectacular**.

17. The word is **intensified**. *The smell of burning intensified as we got closer to the blaze.* The word is **intensified**.

18. The word is **subtle**. *There was a subtle taste of ginger in the biscuit.* The word is **subtle**.

19. The word is **thorough**. *We made a thorough search of the garden but still couldn't find the cat.* The word is **thorough**.

20. The word is **monologue**. *A monologue is a speech made by one person.* The word is **monologue**.

Mixed Test 7

1. The word is **terrible**. *There was a terrible mess in the kitchen.* The word is **terrible**.

2. The word is **through**. *Max crawled through the hedge to get the football.* The word is **through**.

3. The word is **trouble**. *We knew we would be in trouble if we didn't get home soon.* The word is **trouble**.

4. The word is **league**. *Our team is at the top of the league.* The word is **league**.

5. The word is **captured**. *The zoo keepers captured the escaped lion.* The word is **captured**.

6. The word is **sensibly**. *We sensibly hung up our wet coats before we sat by the fire.* The word is **sensibly**.

7. The word is **percussion**. *We like the percussion instruments in music lessons best of all.* The word is **percussion**.

8. The word is **admirable**. *Mike's courage in rescuing the dog from the river was admirable.* The word is **admirable**.

9. The word is **miscalculated**. *Our teacher miscalculated the sum.* The word is **miscalculated**.

10. The word is **disconnect**. *We had to disconnect the circuit before we added the switch.* The word is **disconnect**.

11. The word is **economise**. *Mum said it was time to economise as her pay had been cut.* The word is **economise**.

12. The word is **reversible**. *My new ski jacket is reversible.* The word is **reversible**.

13. The word is **aisle**. *The groom accompanied the bride down the aisle.* The word is **aisle**.

14. The word is **advertise**. *Some companies advertise their products on the television.* The word is **advertise**.

15. The word is **effect**. *The new teacher has had a good effect on our school.* The word is **effect**.

16. The word is **whistle**. *I heard the referee blow the final whistle.* The word is **whistle**.

17. The word is **reassemble**. *Dad showed me how to reassemble the broken model.* The word is **reassemble**.

18. The word is **illegible**. *Grainne's handwriting was totally illegible.* The word is **illegible**.

19. The word is **classified**. *The police said the witness's evidence was classified as top secret.* The word is **classified**.

20. The word is **undeniably**. *Our fans undeniably cheered the loudest.* The word is **undeniably**.

Mixed Test 8

1. The word is **possibly**. *My last birthday was possibly the best day of my life!* The word is **possibly**.

2. The word is **determination**. *Sami approached the diving board full of determination.* The word is **determination**.

3. The word is **excellent**. *Dad had an excellent cup of coffee in the new café.* The word is **excellent**.

4. The word is **mixture**. *There was a good mixture of music at Sophia's party.* The word is **mixture**.

5. The word is **machine**. *My uncle John has bought a new coffee machine.* The word is **machine**.

6. The word is **country**. *You need to show your passport when entering a different country.* The word is **country**.

7. The word is **consequence**. *I had a toothache as a consequence of eating too many sweets.* The word is **consequence**.

8. The word is **incredibly**. *Mum was incredibly disappointed with her new car.* The word is **incredibly**.

9. The word is **operation**. *After her operation, my grandmother was told to rest.* The word is **operation**.

10. The word is **troublesome**. *Liam could be quite troublesome at times.* The word is **troublesome**.

11. The word is **ridiculous**. *The new shoes I wanted were a ridiculous price!* The word is **ridiculous**.

12. The word is **instance**. *In this instance, I agreed with what Ben was saying.* The word is **instance**.

13. The word is **structure**. *The structure of the new building was mainly steel.* The word is **structure**.

14. The word is **conveyed**. *We conveyed our sympathy to Sam when his rabbit died.* The word is **conveyed**.

15. The word is **incompetent**. *Dad said the men who built our extension were incompetent.* The word is **incompetent**.

16. The word is **agency**. *The travel agency rang us to say our tickets were ready for collection.* The word is **agency**.

17. The word is **chauffeur**. *The film star arrived in a limousine driven by a chauffeur.* The word is **chauffeur**.

18. The word is **inferred**. *The author inferred that the hero was finally safe.* The word is **inferred**.

19. The word is **partial**. *Stella is very partial to ice-cream and chocolate sauce.* The word is **partial**.

20. The word is **appearance**. *The appearance of some warmer weather filled us with happiness.* The word is **appearance**.

Mixed Test 9

1. The word is **disagreement**. *After their initial disagreement, Petra and Corel became firm friends.* The word is **disagreement**.

2. The word is **reputation**. *All the schools in our area have a great reputation for good behaviour.* The word is **reputation**.

3. The word is **communication**. *We have a diary for communication between school and home.* The word is **communication**.

4. The word is **misunderstood**. *My teacher misunderstood me when I asked her a question.* The word is **misunderstood**.

5. The word is **ridge**. *We could see the hikers as they approached the ridge.* The word is **ridge**.

6. The word is **signature**. *We needed a signature from our parents to say we could go on the trip.* The word is **signature**.

7. The word is **plague**. *We learned about the plague that caused so many deaths in the seventeenth century.* The word is **plague**.

8. The word is **monarch**. *Queen Elizabeth II is the longest-reigning British monarch.* The word is **monarch**.

9. The word is **negligence**. *The owner's negligence caused the dog to become very ill.* The word is **negligence**.

10. The word is **concussion**. *My cousin suffered from concussion after banging his head in the rugby match.* The word is **concussion**.

11. The word is **visibly**. *Dad was visibly shocked when I told him I got full marks in my maths test.* The word is **visibly**.

12. The word is **synchronise**. *Before the climbers set off, they decided to synchronise their watches.* The word is **synchronise**.

13. The word is **precision**. *With great precision, the doctor stitched the cut on my leg.* The word is **precision**.

14. The word is **resemblance**. *My brother bears a great resemblance to our dad.* The word is **resemblance**.

15. The word is **rendition**. *Clio's rendition of the song was very different to the original version.* The word is **rendition**.

16. The word is **procession**. *There was a colourful procession to celebrate Chinese New Year.* The word is **procession**.

17. The word is **decision**. *The decision to close the school due to the snow was met with delight by the pupils.* The word is **decision**.

18. The word is **condensation**. *The mirror was so steamed up with condensation that I couldn't see my face.* The word is **condensation**.

19. The word is **disposable**. *Most packaging is disposable these days.* The word is **disposable**.

20. The word is **exertion**. *After too much exertion, my grandad gets very tired.* The word is **exertion**.

Mixed Test 10

1. The word is **digestible**. *Vegetables are more easily digestible if they are cooked.* The word is **digestible**.

2. The word is **departure**. *We went on the internet to check our departure time.* The word is **departure**.

3. The word is **special**. *There was a special assembly to say goodbye to Mr Smith, our Deputy Head.* The word is **special**.

4. The word is **rhymes**. *Trouble rhymes with double.* The word is **rhymes**.

5. The word is **synagogue**. *We learned that Jewish people worship in a synagogue.* The word is **synagogue**.

6. The word is **borough**. *The borough where my cousins live has a lot of countryside.* The word is **borough**.

7. The word is **reoccurrence**. *The reoccurrence of my bad cough means I will have to take more medicine.* The word is **reoccurrence**.

8. The word is **occupation**. *My mum has changed her occupation twice in two years.* The word is **occupation**.

9. The word is **conspicuous**. *Our running team was very conspicuous in our bright yellow bibs.* The word is **conspicuous**.

10. The word is **receipt**. *I kept the receipt in case I decided to return my new shoes.* The word is **receipt**.

11. The word is **rough**. *The seas around the island were too rough for the boat to dock.* The word is **rough**.

12. The word is **nudged**. *When the actor forgot his lines, my friend nudged me.* The word is **nudged**.

13. The word is **conference**. *Our Head Teacher enjoyed the conference about healthy eating in schools.* The word is **conference**.

14. The word is **moustache**. *Grandad trims his moustache every week.* The word is **moustache**.

15. The word is **admission**. *My sister paid £5.00 for our admission to the fair.* The word is **admission**.

16. The word is **chemist**. *We went to the chemist to buy plasters.* The word is **chemist**.

17. The word is **incidence**. *There has been an increased incidence of littering in the playground.* The word is **incidence**.

18. The word is **seized**. *The athlete seized the winning trophy and ran around the track.* The word is **seized**.

19. The word is **tension**. *There was a lot of tension in the air when Dad burnt the dinner.* The word is **tension**.

20. The word is **conscious**. *Sami was conscious that Archie didn't have a partner.* The word is **conscious**.

Mixed Test 11

1. The word is **vegetable**. *My grandad made a chicken and vegetable pie.* The word is **vegetable**.

2. The word is **identification**. *Before we could cross the border, we had to show our identification papers.* The word is **identification**.

3. The word is **custom**. *Where I live, it is a local custom to have a treasure hunt every summer.* The word is **custom**.

4. The word is **dictionary**. *Our teacher encourages us to use a dictionary for words we find difficult to spell.* The word is **dictionary**.

5. The word is **envelope**. *I placed the invitation card in an envelope and put it in the post box.* The word is **envelope**.

6. The word is **temperature**. *Charlie's mum took his temperature when he had the flu.* The word is **temperature**.

7. The word is **permanent**. *Unfortunately, the ink stain on the carpet was permanent.* The word is **permanent**.

8. The word is **tongue**. *The drink left a bitter taste on my tongue.* The word is **tongue**.

9. The word is **persuasive**. *Grace was very persuasive when it came to asking for extra pocket money.* The word is **persuasive**.

10. The word is **production**. *The teachers discussed our end of year production.* The word is **production**.

11. The word is **eligible**. *Anyone who had not been elected before was eligible for membership of the school committee.* The word is **eligible**.

12. The word is **technology**. *There has been a massive advance in modern technology in the last twenty years.* The word is **technology**.

13. The word is **exaggeration**. *My best friend tells great stories which are full of exaggeration.* The word is **exaggeration**.

14. The word is **aggression**. *The robber reacted with aggression when arrested by the police.* The word is **aggression**.

15. The word is **hymn**. *We helped to choose a hymn for the wedding.* The word is **hymn**.

16. The word is **ledge**. *Mum left a spare key on the ledge.* The word is **ledge**.

17. The word is **immediate**. *There was immediate applause when Nick finished singing.* The word is **immediate**.

18. The word is **controversial**. *The suggestion by the Head Teacher to change the school uniform was very controversial.* The word is **controversial**.

19. The word is **equipped**. *The climbers were equipped with remote control radios as a safety measure.* The word is **equipped**.

20. The word is **chute**. *Our favourite ride at the activity centre was the water chute.* The word is **chute**.

Mixed Test 12

1. The word is **important**. *It is important to keep yourself physically fit.* The word is **important**.

2. The word is **condition**. *Dad's new car is second-hand but in great condition.* The word is **condition**.

3. The word is **familiar**. *The familiar face we spotted at the airport turned out to be our neighbour's.* The word is **familiar**.

4. The word is **considerable**. *There was a considerable amount of rain last night.* The word is **considerable**.

5. The word is **bough**. *Sitting on the tree's bough were four little blue tits.* The word is **bough**.

6. The word is **available**. *There were no more parking spaces available so we parked on the grass.* The word is **available**.

7. The word is **restaurant**. *We went to a vegetarian restaurant to celebrate Emily's birthday.* The word is **restaurant**.

8. The word is **symbol**. *A crab is the astrological symbol for the zodiac sign Cancer.* The word is **symbol**.

9. The word is **decently**. *The prisoners were treated decently by the guards.* The word is **decently**.

10. The word is **fractured**. *The doctor said I had fractured my wrist.* The word is **fractured**.

11. The word is **obedient**. *We knew we hadn't been very obedient so we deserved to lose our break.* The word is **obedient**.

12. The word is **technicians**. *Two technicians came to school to fix our computer problems.* The word is **technicians**.

13. The word is **session**. *We enjoyed our extra gymnastics session this morning.* The word is **session**.

14. The word is **opaque**. *The opposite of transparent is **opaque**.* The word is **opaque**.

15. The word is **smudged**. *I **smudged** my writing because the ink was still wet.* The word is **smudged**.

16. The word is **awkward**. *There was an **awkward** silence when Faiz told the teacher he hadn't done his homework again.* The word is **awkward**.

17. The word is **correspondence**. *We read the **correspondence** between a soldier in World War II and his family.* The word is **correspondence**.

18. The word is **nuisance**. *The new puppy was a **nuisance** when Zachary was trying to play football.* The word is **nuisance**.

19. The word is **exaggerating**. *Susie thought Mike was **exaggerating** when he said he had been chosen to sing for the Queen.* The word is **exaggerating**.

20. The word is **leisure**. *The new **leisure** complex has an amazing trampoline.* The word is **leisure**.

Mixed Test 13

1. The word is **respectable**. *The mayor is a **respectable** and hard-working member of our community.* The word is **respectable**.

2. The word is **certainly**. *Our trip to the seaside was **certainly** one of the best days of the holidays.* The word is **certainly**.

3. The word is **extension**. *When the new baby arrives, we will need to build an **extension**.* The word is **extension**.

4. The word is **type**. *We are learning to **type** without looking at the keyboard.* The word is **type**.

5. The word is **relevant**. *The **relevant** people were informed about the break-in.* The word is **relevant**.

6. The word is **pronunciation**. *The **pronunciation** of certain words can differ depending on dialects.* The word is **pronunciation**.

7. The word is **distance**. *It is quite a **distance** from home to school so we travel by car.* The word is **distance**.

8. The word is **opportunities**. *Ahmed had many **opportunities** to apologise.* The word is **opportunities**.

9. The word is **stomach**. *If I eat a lot of chocolate, my **stomach** starts to hurt.* The word is **stomach**.

10. The word is **frequency**. *The increased **frequency** of rain in British summers has meant more people travel abroad.* The word is **frequency**.

11. The word is **venture**. *Dad's new business **venture** was a big success.* The word is **venture**.

12. The word is **parachute**. *The pilot used his **parachute** to eject safely from the plane.* The word is **parachute**.

13. The word is **siege**. *We followed the dramatic **siege** on the news last night.* The word is **siege**.

14. The word is **featured**. *The TV chat show **featured** my favourite actor.* The word is **featured**.

15. The word is **trough**. *On our class trip to the farm, we watched the pigs feeding from a **trough**.* The word is **trough**.

16. The word is **rogue**. *The main character in the film was a loveable **rogue**.* The word is **rogue**.

17. The word is **parliamentary**. *My parents like to listen to **parliamentary** debates on the radio.* The word is **parliamentary**.

18. The word is **leisurely**. *I walked **leisurely** down the country lane.* The word is **leisurely**.

19. The word is **interference**. *The **interference** on the radio meant we couldn't hear the music properly.* The word is **interference**.

20. The word is **categories**. *In science, we put the animals into different **categories**.* The word is **categories**.

Mixed Test 14

1. The word is **explanation**. *Ciara was asked to give an **explanation** about the state of her bedroom.* The word is **explanation**.

2. The word is **programme**. *My favourite television **programme** is on too late during term time.* The word is **programme**.

3. The word is **weird**. *Stan and Harvey made some **weird** but wonderful models out of clay.* The word is **weird**.

4. The word is **fridge**. *I opened the **fridge** to find that it was almost empty.* The word is **fridge**.

5. The word is **muscles**. *My **muscles** felt tight as I hadn't exercised for some time.* The word is **muscles**.

6. The word is **queue**. *We stood in the **queue** for an hour before finally entering the theme park.* The word is **queue**.

7. The word is **anchor**. *The captain dropped the **anchor** close to the shore.* The word is **anchor**.

8. The word is **fixtures**. *There are two important rugby **fixtures** this weekend.* The word is **fixtures**.

9. The word is **unnecessary**. *The nurse said it was quite **unnecessary** to thank her for her help.* The word is **unnecessary**.

10. The word is **acceptance**. *We sent a reply in **acceptance** of the party invitation.* The word is **acceptance**.

11. The word is **disruption**. *The strike by the train drivers caused a major **disruption**.* The word is **disruption**.

12. The word is **generous**. *Ted made a **generous** donation to the animal charity.* The word is **generous**.

13. The word is **mathematician**. *Max is an excellent **mathematician**.* The word is **mathematician**.

14. The word is **cymbals**. *I crashed the **cymbals** while Millie banged the drums.* The word is **cymbals**.

15. The word is **variety**. *There was a **variety** of ice-cream on sale at the fair.* The word is **variety**.

16. The word is **language**. *Learning a **language** can help you communicate when you are abroad.* The word is **language**.

17. The word is **brilliance**. *The **brilliance** of the shining stars at night has always fascinated me.* The word is **brilliance**.

18. The word is **occupied**. *Zuma was **occupied** with her own, private thoughts.* The word is **occupied**.

19. The word is **sufficiently**. *I don't think we tidied up **sufficiently** as Mum looked a bit grumpy.* The word is **sufficiently**.

20. The word is **cheque**. *The teacher asked us for a **cheque** to pay for our trip to the museum.* The word is **cheque**.

Mixed Test 15

1. The word is **recommended**. *My teacher **recommended** that I practise my times tables more often.* The word is **recommended**.

2. The word is **coughed**. *I coughed all night despite the medicine Mum gave me.* The word is **coughed**.

3. The word is **ridge**. *On the mountain ridge stood a majestic deer.* The word is **ridge**.

4. The word is **achievement**. *The marathon runners were very proud of their achievement.* The word is **achievement**.

5. The word is **shoulder**. *I dislocated my shoulder when I fell off the horse.* The word is **shoulder**.

6. The word is **future**. *In future, I will write a note to remind me to bring my PE kit to school.* The word is **future**.

7. The word is **unveil**. *The celebrity was asked to unveil the statue in the centre of town.* The word is **unveil**.

8. The word is **choir**. *The choir sang beautifully last night.* The word is **choir**.

9. The word is **occurred**. *It occurred to me that I hadn't said happy birthday to my cousin.* The word is **occurred**.

10. The word is **electrician**. *The electrician soon had our lights working again.* The word is **electrician**.

11. The word is **consideration**. *In consideration of our neighbours, we turned down the music at our party.* The word is **consideration**.

12. The word is **sympathy**. *I couldn't help but feel sympathy for the puppy when he was told off.* The word is **sympathy**.

13. The word is **government**. *The government elections will take place in May.* The word is **government**.

14. The word is **existence**. *Victorian children who lived in a workhouse had a difficult existence.* The word is **existence**.

15. The word is **professional**. *Our parents agreed that our class performance was very professional.* The word is **professional**.

16. The word is **dangerous**. *It was decided that it was too dangerous to climb the mountain in the fog.* The word is **dangerous**.

17. The word is **foreigner**. *The foreigner asked us to help him find his hotel.* The word is **foreigner**.

18. The word is **curiosity**. *The arrival of a limousine caused much curiosity in our neighbourhood.* The word is **curiosity**.

19. The word is **recognition**. *Some artists only get the recognition they deserve after they have died.* The word is **recognition**.

20. The word is **conscience**. *My conscience told me to give the homeless lady some money.* The word is **conscience**.

Mixed Test 16

1. The word is **their**. *Mum and Dad decided to change their car.* The word is **their**.

2. The word is **horribly**. *After a horribly wet weekend, we finally saw some sunshine on Monday.* The word is **horribly**.

3. The word is **according**. *There has been a gas explosion at the factory, according to the news.* The word is **according**.

4. The word is **parliament**. *The parliament building in London is very impressive.* The word is **parliament**.

5. The word is **fudge**. *Gran's favourite sweet is fudge.* The word is **fudge**.

6. The word is **apparent**. *There was no apparent problem with my tooth despite the pain I'd been having.* The word is **apparent**.

7. The word is **average**. *My big brother is average in height but has very big feet.* The word is **average**.

8. The word is **soldier**. *The soldier received a special award for his outstanding bravery.* The word is **soldier**.

9. The word is **delicious**. *We had the most delicious homemade pizza this evening.* The word is **delicious**.

10. The word is **ancient**. *The ancient city of Rome has many interesting sites.* The word is **ancient**.

11. The word is **system**. *Our teacher has a special system for marking our work.* The word is **system**.

12. The word is **culture**. *In British culture, tea is a very popular drink.* The word is **culture**.

13. The word is **chaos**. *When the winning trophy was displayed to the crowds, chaos erupted.* The word is **chaos**.

14. The word is **residence**. *The Prime Minister's residence is in Downing Street, London.* The word is **residence**.

15. The word is **thoroughly**. *We were thoroughly drenched by the time we got home.* The word is **thoroughly**.

16. The word is **beige**. *On safari, we wore mainly beige and green clothes as camouflage.* The word is **beige**.

17. The word is **cemetery**. *The cemetery had many ancient gravestones.* The word is **cemetery**.

18. The word is **annoyance**. *It was with great annoyance that I helped Mum weed the garden while the others were playing.* The word is **annoyance**.

19. The word is **accompanied**. *Zainab accompanied Flo to the cinema yesterday.* The word is **accompanied**.

20. The word is **crucial**. *It is crucial to drink a lot of water when walking in hot temperatures.* The word is **crucial**.

Mixed Test 17

1. The word is **programme**. *We watched an interesting programme on television last night.* The word is **programme**.

2. The word is **naturally**. *Edward and Millie were naturally very upset when their guinea pig was ill.* The word is **naturally**.

3. The word is **official**. *The Queen celebrates her official birthday in June each year.* The word is **official**.

4. The word is **increasingly**. *There are increasingly more accidents on the road going into town.* The word is **increasingly**.

5. The word is **recommend**. *Harry said he would definitely recommend a holiday in Spain.* The word is **recommend**.

6. The word is **peculiar**. *Seb found a peculiar insect in the garden shed.* The word is **peculiar**.

7. The word is **typical**. *It was typical of Mair to ruin the game.* The word is **typical**.

8. The word is **ached**. *My muscles ached after the gymnastics session.* The word is **ached**.

9. The word is **eighteenth**. *For her eighteenth birthday, Chloe was given a gold bracelet.* The word is **eighteenth**.

10. The word is **attached**. *Dad found a cheque attached to the letter from the insurance company.* The word is **attached**.

11. The word is **ordinarily**. *We took the bus, although ordinarily we would walk.* The word is **ordinarily**.

12. The word is **scheme**. *Our school has introduced a scheme to encourage children to learn their spellings.* The word is **scheme**.

13. The word is **committee**. *The local environment committee decided more needed to be done about litter in our area.* The word is **committee**.

14. The word is **inconceivable**. *Mum said it was inconceivable that Tim had started the argument in the playground.* The word is **inconceivable**.

15. The word is **literature**. *Shakespeare is one of the best-known writers of literature in the world.* The word is **literature**.

16. The word is **secretary**. *The school secretary keeps a record of our absences.* The word is **secretary**.

17. The word is **physical**. *Doing some physical exercise each day is important to stay fit, healthy and strong.* The word is **physical**.

18. The word is **curious**. *We were curious about the large parcel on the table.* The word is **curious.**

19. The word is **precious**. *Every moment spent with my old grandad is very precious.* The word is **precious.**

20. The word is **plaque**. *The mayor presented a plaque in memory of the famous tennis player.* The word is **plaque**.

Mixed Test 18

1. The word is **ought**. *We ought to get all our spellings correct as we have practised hard.* The word is **ought**.

2. The word is **royal**. *The royal parade marched down the long, red carpet.* The word is **royal**.

3. The word is **equipment**. *On our camping trip, we had all the necessary equipment to cook meals.* The word is **equipment**.

4. The word is **determination**. *Sir Edmund Hillary's determination enabled him to reach the summit of Mount Everest.* The word is **determination**.

5. The word is **historical**. *I like reading historical novels best of all.* The word is **historical**.

6. The word is **aggressive**. *When he is hungry, my cat can be quite aggressive.* The word is **aggressive**.

7. The word is **feature**. *Some people think my hair is my best feature.* The word is **feature**.

8. The word is **occasionally**. *There are occasionally protests about pollution in our local area.* The word is **occasionally**.

9. The word is **opposition**. *Unfortunately, the opposition scored against us in the last minute.* The word is **opposition**.

10. The word is **average**. *The average age at Grandad's birthday party was sixty-seven.* The word is **average**.

11. The word is **furious**. *Ellen was furious when Mo ate her last crisp!* The word is **furious**.

12. The word is **interruptions**. *The constant interruptions were annoying our teacher.* The word is **interruptions**.

13. The word is **circumference**. *The circumference of a circle is the distance round the edge.* The word is **circumference**.

14. The word is **criticising**. *After criticising my homework, my sister apologised and helped me rewrite it.* The word is **criticising**.

15. The word is **controversy**. *There was a lot of controversy about building a motorway so close to our town.* The word is **controversy**.

16. The word is **yacht**. *My aunt sails her yacht around the Isles of Scilly every summer.* The word is **yacht**.

17. The word is **cautiously**. *Finn walked cautiously along the cliff path.* The word is **cautiously**.

18. The word is **grammatically**. *I checked that my sentence was grammatically correct.* The word is **grammatically**.

19. The word is **grotesque**. *The monster's face was so grotesque that the princess screamed in horror.* The word is **grotesque**.

20. The word is **convenience**. *Mum was told she could meet the bank manager at her convenience.* The word is **convenience**.

Mixed Test 19

1. The word is **competition**. *The Year 6 singing competition was a great success.* The word is **competition**.

2. The word is **forty**. *It's hard to believe that my mum was born only forty years after the end of World War II.* The word is **forty**.

3. The word is **embarrassing**. *It was very embarrassing when I realised I'd forgotten my best friend's birthday.* The word is **embarrassing**.

4. The word is **appreciation**. *We showed our appreciation for the excellent performance by standing up and clapping.* The word is **appreciation**.

5. The word is **communication**. *The lack of communication between Ryan and his sister meant they were late for the party.* The word is **communication**.

6. The word is **architect**. *Bill would like to be an architect like his grandfather.* The word is **architect**.

7. The word is **conveniently**. *Nishwa was conveniently missing when we were asked to tidy up the classroom.* The word is **conveniently**.

8. The word is **tradition**. *It is a tradition in our family to have a party on New Year's Eve.* The word is **tradition**.

9. The word is **persuade**. *Sabrina tried hard to persuade her mum to take her to the shops.* The word is **persuade**.

10. The word is **symbolises**. *In our class, a red square placed on the board symbolises 'no talking'.* The word is **symbolises**.

11. The word is **interfering**. *The constant rain was interfering with our plans to go on a picnic.* The word is **interfering**.

12. The word is **sculpture**. *We took photographs of the sculpture at the museum so we could study it further at school.* The word is **sculpture**.

13. The word is **chorus**. *In the summer, a chorus of noisy birds wakes me up every morning.* The word is **chorus**.

14. The word is **sediment**. *There was a layer of sediment at the bottom of the jar.* The word is **sediment**.

15. The word is **gorgeous**. *Flo's gorgeous new puppy nipped my fingers.* The word is **gorgeous**.

16. The word is **heir**. *The heir to the throne is learning how to perform royal duties.* The word is **heir**.

17. The word is **muscular**. *The muscular weightlifter won the champion's trophy.* The word is **muscular**.

18. The word is **prejudice**. *Nelson Mandela did a lot to stop prejudice against black people in South Africa.* The word is **prejudice**.

19. The word is **familiarity**. *After a long holiday, I always enjoy the familiarity of home.* The word is **familiarity**.

20. The word is **referral**. *The doctor gave me a referral to the hospital when I injured my wrist.* The word is **referral**.

Mixed Test 20

1. The word is **expedition**. *The exhausted explorers were relieved when their expedition came to an end.* The word is **expedition**.

2. The word is **recommended**. *It is important not to exceed the recommended dose.* The word is **recommended**.

3. The word is **mysterious**. *There was a mysterious figure walking in the fog.* The word is **mysterious**.

4. The word is **artificial**. *My mum bought an artificial Christmas tree.* The word is **artificial**.

5. The word is **especially**. *It is especially hard to believe that we will be in secondary school soon.* The word is **especially**.

6. The word is **substance**. *Matt and Gem stirred the substance until it melted.* The word is **substance**.

7. The word is **discussion**. *Mum and Dad were having a discussion.* The word is **discussion**.

8. The word is **religious**. *The religious leaders met to discuss ways to help the homeless in our country.* The word is **religious**.

9. The word is **corresponded**. *The two friends corresponded with each other by post.* The word is **corresponded**.

10. The word is **outweighed**. *We decided the good points about school outweighed the bad points.* The word is **outweighed**.

11. The word is **definition**. *The definition in Zara's sketch was excellent.* The word is **definition**.

12. The word is **hazardous**. *After a rather hazardous journey, we arrived safely in the snowy mountains.* The word is **hazardous**.

13. The word is **efficient**. *If we are not efficient in how we use energy, we will have huge bills to pay.* The word is **efficient**.

14. The word is **convenient**. *It was quite convenient that we met Maire as she was able to give us a lift home.* The word is **convenient**.

15. The word is **oxygen**. *At the summit of Mount Everest, the air is thin as there is less oxygen.* The word is **oxygen**.

16. The word is **mechanic**. *Our mechanic told us our car needed a new battery.* The word is **mechanic**.

17. The word is **monstrous**. *The monstrous behaviour of Callum resulted in the whole class staying behind at lunchtime.* The word is **monstrous**.

18. The word is **height**. *At the height of his career, Alfred earned more money in a day than most people earned in a year.* The word is **height**.

19. The word is **chronological**. *After our trip to the museum, we were asked to write a chronological report.* The word is **chronological**.

20. The word is **immature**. *Although he can be quite immature, my brother is usually kind to me.* The word is **immature**.

11 Mum said it was time to _____ as her pay had been cut.

1 mark

12 My new ski jacket is _____.

1 mark

13 The groom accompanied the bride down the _____.

1 mark

14 Some companies _____ their products on the television.

1 mark

15 The new teacher has had a good _____ on our school.

1 mark

16 I heard the referee blow the final _____.

1 mark

17 Dad showed me how to _____ the broken model.

1 mark

18 Grainne's handwriting was totally _____.

1 mark

19 The police said the witness's evidence was _____ as top secret.

1 mark

20 Our fans _____ cheered the loudest.

1 mark

Total marks .... /20   How am I doing?

Mixed Test 8

Listen carefully to the missing word and fill in the answer space.

1 My last birthday was _____ the best day of my life! 1 mark

2 Sami approached the diving board full of _____. 1 mark

3 Dad had an _____ cup of coffee in the new café. 1 mark

4 There was a good _____ of music at Sophia's party. 1 mark

5 My uncle John has bought a new coffee _____. 1 mark

6 You need to show your passport when entering a

different _____. 1 mark

7 I had a toothache as a _____ of eating too many
sweets. 1 mark

8 Mum was _____ disappointed with her new car. 1 mark

9 After her _____, my grandmother was told to rest. 1 mark

10 Liam could be quite _____ at times. 1 mark

11 The new shoes I wanted were a _____ price!

12 In this _____, I agreed with what Ben was saying.

13 The _____ of the new building was mainly steel.

14 We _____ our sympathy to Sam when his rabbit died.

15 Dad said the men who built our extension were

_____.

16 The travel _____ rang us to say our tickets were ready for collection.

17 The film star arrived in a limousine driven by a _____.

18 The author _____ that the hero was finally safe.

19 Stella is very _____ to ice-cream and chocolate sauce.

20 The _____ of some warmer weather filled us with happiness.

Total marks .... /20   How am I doing? 😊 😐 😣

Mixed Test 9

Listen carefully to the missing word and fill in the answer space.

1 After their initial _____, Petra and Corel became
firm friends.

1 mark

2 All the schools in our area have a great _____ for
good behaviour.

1 mark

3 We have a diary for _____ between school and home.

1 mark

4 My teacher _____ me when I asked her a question.

1 mark

5 We could see the hikers as they approached the

_____.

1 mark

6 We needed a _____ from our parents to say we
could go on the trip.

1 mark

7 We learned about the _____ that caused so many
deaths in the seventeenth century.

1 mark

8 Queen Elizabeth II is the longest-reigning British _____.

1 mark

9 The owner's _____ caused the dog to become
very ill.

1 mark

10 My cousin suffered from _____ after banging his head
in the rugby match.

1 mark

11 Dad was _____ shocked when I told him I got full

marks in my maths test.

1 mark

12 Before the climbers set off, they decided to _____

their watches.

1 mark

13 With great _____, the doctor stitched the cut on

my leg.

1 mark

14 My brother bears a great _____ to our dad.

1 mark

15 Clio's _____ of the song was very different to the

original version.

1 mark

16 There was a colourful _____ to celebrate Chinese

New Year.

1 mark

17 The _____ to close the school due to the snow

was met with delight by the pupils.

1 mark

18 The mirror was so steamed up with _____ that I

couldn't see my face.

1 mark

19 Most packaging is _____ these days.

1 mark

20 After too much _____, my grandad gets very tired.

1 mark

Total marks .... /20   How am I doing? ☺ 😐 ☹

Mixed Test 10

Listen carefully to the missing word and fill in the answer space.

1 Vegetables are more easily _____ if they are cooked.

1 mark

2 We went on the internet to check our _____ time.

1 mark

3 There was a _____ assembly to say goodbye to Mr Smith, our Deputy Head.

1 mark

4 Trouble _____ with double.

1 mark

5 We learned that Jewish people worship in a _____.

1 mark

6 The _____ where my cousins live has a lot of countryside.

1 mark

7 The _____ of my bad cough means I will have to take more medicine.

1 mark

8 My mum has changed her _____ twice in two years.

1 mark

9 Our running team was very _____ in our bright yellow bibs.

1 mark

10 I kept the _____ in case I decided to return my new shoes.

1 mark

11 The seas around the island were too _____ for the boat to dock.

12 When the actor forgot his lines, my friend _____ me.

13 Our Head Teacher enjoyed the _____ about healthy eating in schools.

14 Grandad trims his _____ every week.

15 My sister paid £5.00 for our _____ to the fair.

16 We went to the _____ to buy plasters.

17 There has been an increased _____ of littering in the playground.

18 The athlete _____ the winning trophy and ran around the track.

19 There was a lot of _____ in the air when Dad burnt the dinner.

20 Sami was _____ that Archie didn't have a partner.

Total marks .... /20   How am I doing? 😊 😐 😞

Mixed Test II

Listen carefully to the missing word and fill in the answer space.

1 My grandad made a chicken and _____ pie.

2 Before we could cross the border, we had to show

our _____ papers.

3 Where I live, it is a local _____ to have a treasure hunt every summer.

4 Our teacher encourages us to use a _____ for words we find difficult to spell.

5 I placed the invitation card in an _____ and put it in the post box.

6 Charlie's mum took his _____ when he had the flu.

7 Unfortunately, the ink stain on the carpet was _____.

8 The drink left a bitter taste on my _____.

9 Grace was very _____ when it came to asking for extra pocket money.

10 The teachers discussed our end of year _____.

11 Anyone who had not been elected before was _____
for membership of the school committee.

1 mark

12 There has been a massive advance in modern _____
in the last twenty years.

1 mark

13 My best friend tells great stories which are full of

_____.

1 mark

14 The robber reacted with _____ when arrested by
the police.

1 mark

15 We helped to choose a _____ for the wedding.

1 mark

16 Mum left a spare key on the _____.

1 mark

17 There was _____ applause when Nick finished
singing.

1 mark

18 The suggestion by the Head Teacher to change the school uniform

was very _____.

1 mark

19 The climbers were _____ with remote control
radios as a safety measure.

1 mark

20 Our favourite ride at the activity centre was the water _____. 1 mark

Total marks .... /20   How am I doing? ☺ 😐 ☹

Mixed Test 12

Listen carefully to the missing word and fill in the answer space.

1 It is _____ to keep yourself physically fit. 1 mark

2 Dad's new car is second-hand but in great _____. 1 mark

3 The _____ face we spotted at the airport turned out to be our neighbour's. 1 mark

4 There was a _____ amount of rain last night. 1 mark

5 Sitting on the tree's _____ were four little blue tits. 1 mark

6 There were no more parking spaces _____ so we parked on the grass. 1 mark

7 We went to a vegetarian _____ to celebrate Emily's birthday. 1 mark

8 A crab is the astrological _____ for the zodiac sign Cancer. 1 mark

9 The prisoners were treated _____ by the guards. 1 mark

10 The doctor said I had _____ my wrist. 1 mark

11 We knew we hadn't been very _____ so we deserved to lose our break.

1 mark

12 Two _____ came to school to fix our computer problems.

1 mark

13 We enjoyed our extra gymnastics _____ this morning.

1 mark

14 The opposite of transparent is _____.

1 mark

15 I _____ my writing because the ink was still wet.

1 mark

16 There was an _____ silence when Faiz told the teacher he hadn't done his homework again.

1 mark

17 We read the _____ between a soldier in World War II and his family.

1 mark

18 The new puppy was a _____ when Zachary was trying to play football.

1 mark

19 Susie thought Mike was _____ when he said he had been chosen to sing for the Queen.

1 mark

20 The new _____ complex has an amazing trampoline.

1 mark

Total marks .... /20   How am I doing? 😊 😐 ☹

Mixed Test 13

Listen carefully to the missing word and fill in the answer space.

1 The mayor is a _____ and hard-working member
of our community.

1 mark

2 Our trip to the seaside was _____ one of the best
days of the holidays.

1 mark

3 When the new baby arrives, we will need to build an

_____.

1 mark

4 We are learning to _____ without looking at the
keyboard.

1 mark

5 The _____ people were informed about the break-in.

1 mark

6 The _____ of certain words can differ depending
on dialects.

1 mark

7 It is quite a _____ from home to school so we
travel by car.

1 mark

8 Ahmed had many _____ to apologise.

1 mark

9 If I eat a lot of chocolate, my _____ starts to hurt.

1 mark

10 The increased _____ of rain in British summers
has meant more people travel abroad.

1 mark

11 Dad's new business _____ was a big success.

1 mark

12 The pilot used his _____ to eject safely from the plane.

1 mark

13 We followed the dramatic _____ on the news last night.

1 mark

14 The TV chat show _____ my favourite actor.

1 mark

15 On our class trip to the farm, we watched the pigs feeding from

a _____.

1 mark

16 The main character in the film was a loveable _____.

1 mark

17 My parents like to listen to _____ debates on the radio.

1 mark

18 I walked _____ down the country lane.

1 mark

19 The _____ on the radio meant we couldn't hear the music properly.

1 mark

20 In science, we put the animals into different _____.

1 mark

Total marks .... /20   How am I doing? ☺ ☺ ☹

Mixed Test 14

Listen carefully to the missing word and fill in the answer space.

1 Ciara was asked to give an _____ about the state of her bedroom.

1 mark

2 My favourite television _____ is on too late during term time.

1 mark

3 Stan and Harvey made some _____ but wonderful models out of clay.

1 mark

4 I opened the _____ to find that it was almost empty.

1 mark

5 My _____ felt tight as I hadn't exercised for some time.

1 mark

6 We stood in the _____ for an hour before finally entering the theme park.

1 mark

7 The captain dropped the _____ close to the shore.

1 mark

8 There are two important rugby _____ this weekend.

1 mark

9 The nurse said it was quite _____ to thank her for her help.

1 mark

10 We sent a reply in _____ of the party invitation.

1 mark

44

11 The strike by the train drivers caused a major _____. 1 mark

12 Ted made a _____ donation to the animal charity. 1 mark

13 Max is an excellent _____. 1 mark

14 I crashed the _____ while Millie banged the drums. 1 mark

15 There was a _____ of ice-cream on sale at the fair. 1 mark

16 Learning a _____ can help you communicate when you are abroad. 1 mark

17 The _____ of the shining stars at night has always fascinated me. 1 mark

18 Zuma was _____ with her own, private thoughts. 1 mark

19 I don't think we tidied up _____ as Mum looked a bit grumpy. 1 mark

20 The teacher asked us for a _____ to pay for our trip to the museum. 1 mark

Total marks .... /20   How am I doing?

Mixed Test 15

Listen carefully to the missing word and fill in the answer space.

1 My teacher _____ that I practise my times tables
more often.

2 I _____ all night despite the medicine Mum gave me.

3 On the mountain _____ stood a majestic deer.

4 The marathon runners were very proud of their _____.

5 I dislocated my _____ when I fell off the horse.

6 In _____, I will write a note to remind me to bring
my PE kit to school.

7 The celebrity was asked to _____ the statue in the
centre of town.

8 The _____ sang beautifully last night.

9 It _____ to me that I hadn't said happy birthday to
my cousin.

10 The _____ soon had our lights working again.

11 In _____ of our neighbours, we turned down the
music at our party.

12 I couldn't help but feel _____ for the puppy when he was told off.

1 mark

13 The _____ elections will take place in May.

1 mark

14 Victorian children who lived in a workhouse had a

difficult _____.

1 mark

15 Our parents agreed that our class performance was

very _____.

1 mark

16 It was decided that it was too _____ to climb the mountain in the fog.

1 mark

17 The _____ asked us to help him find his hotel.

1 mark

18 The arrival of a limousine caused much _____ in our neighbourhood.

1 mark

19 Some artists only get the _____ they deserve after they have died.

1 mark

20 My _____ told me to give the homeless lady some money.

1 mark

Total marks .... /20   How am I doing? 😊   😐   😣

Mixed Test 16

Listen carefully to the missing word and fill in the answer space.

1 Mum and Dad decided to change _____ car.

2 After a _____ wet weekend, we finally saw some sunshine on Monday.

3 There has been a gas explosion at the factory, _____ to the news.

4 The _____ building in London is very impressive.

5 Gran's favourite sweet is _____.

6 There was no _____ problem with my tooth despite the pain I'd been having.

7 My big brother is _____ in height but has very big feet.

8 The _____ received a special award for his outstanding bravery.

9 We had the most _____ homemade pizza this evening.

10 The _____ city of Rome has many interesting sites.

11 Our teacher has a special _____ for marking our work. 1 mark

12 In British _____, tea is a very popular drink. 1 mark

13 When the winning trophy was displayed to the crowds,

_____ erupted. 1 mark

14 The Prime Minister's _____ is in Downing Street, London. 1 mark

15 We were _____ drenched by the time we got home. 1 mark

16 On safari, we wore mainly _____ and green clothes as camouflage. 1 mark

17 The _____ had many ancient gravestones. 1 mark

18 It was with great _____ that I helped Mum weed the garden while the others were playing. 1 mark

19 Zainab _____ Flo to the cinema yesterday. 1 mark

20 It is _____ to drink a lot of water when walking in hot temperatures. 1 mark

Total marks .... /20   How am I doing? ☺ ☺ ☹

Mixed Test 17

Listen carefully to the missing word and fill in the answer space.

1 We watched an interesting _____ on television last night.

2 Edward and Millie were _____ very upset when their guinea pig was ill.

3 The Queen celebrates her _____ birthday in June each year.

4 There are _____ more accidents on the road going into town.

5 Harry said he would definitely _____ a holiday in Spain.

6 Seb found a _____ insect in the garden shed.

7 It was _____ of Mair to ruin the game.

8 My muscles _____ after the gymnastics session.

9 For her _____ birthday, Chloe was given a gold bracelet.

10 Dad found a cheque _____ to the letter from the insurance company.

11 We took the bus, although _____ we would walk. 1 mark

12 Our school has introduced a _____ to encourage children to learn their spellings. 1 mark

13 The local environment _____ decided more needed to be done about litter in our area. 1 mark

14 Mum said it was _____ that Tim had started the argument in the playground. 1 mark

15 Shakespeare is one of the best-known writers of _____ in the world. 1 mark

16 The school _____ keeps a record of our absences. 1 mark

17 Doing some _____ exercise each day is important to stay fit, healthy and strong. 1 mark

18 We were _____ about the large parcel on the table. 1 mark

19 Every moment spent with my old grandad is very

_____. 1 mark

20 The mayor presented a _____ in memory of the famous tennis player. 1 mark

Total marks .... /20   How am I doing?

Listen carefully to the missing word and fill in the answer space.

1 We _____ to get all our spellings correct as we
have practised hard.

1 mark

2 The _____ parade marched down the long,
red carpet.

1 mark

3 On our camping trip, we had all the necessary _____
to cook meals.

1 mark

4 Sir Edmund Hillary's _____ enabled him to reach
the summit of Mount Everest.

1 mark

5 I like reading _____ novels best of all.

1 mark

6 When he is hungry, my cat can be quite _____.

1 mark

7 Some people think my hair is my best _____.

1 mark

8 There are _____ protests about pollution in our
local area.

1 mark

9 Unfortunately, the _____ scored against us in the
last minute.

1 mark

10 The _____ age at Grandad's birthday party was
sixty-seven.

1 mark

11 Ellen was _____ when Mo ate her last crisp!   1 mark

12 The constant _____ were annoying our teacher.   1 mark

13 The _____ of a circle is the distance round the edge.   1 mark

14 After _____ my homework, my sister apologised and helped me rewrite it.   1 mark

15 There was a lot of _____ about building a motorway so close to our town.   1 mark

16 My aunt sails her _____ around the Isles of Scilly every summer.   1 mark

17 Finn walked _____ along the cliff path.   1 mark

18 I checked that my sentence was _____ correct.   1 mark

19 The monster's face was so _____ that the princess screamed in horror.   1 mark

20 Mum was told she could meet the bank manager at

her _____.   1 mark

Total marks .... /20   How am I doing? 😊 😐 😣

Mixed Test 19

Listen carefully to the missing word and fill in the answer space.

1 The Year 6 singing _____ was a great success.

2 It's hard to believe that my mum was born only

_____ years after the end of World War II.

3 It was very _____ when I realised I'd forgotten my best friend's birthday.

4 We showed our _____ for the excellent performance by standing up and clapping.

5 The lack of _____ between Ryan and his sister meant they were late for the party.

6 Bill would like to be an _____ like his grandfather.

7 Nishwa was _____ missing when we were asked to tidy up the classroom.

8 It is a _____ in our family to have a party on New Year's Eve.

9 Sabrina tried hard to _____ her mum to take her to the shops.

10 In our class, a red square placed on the board _____ 'no talking'.

11 The constant rain was _____ with our plans to go
on a picnic.

1 mark

12 We took photographs of the _____ at the museum
so we could study it further at school.

1 mark

13 In the summer, a _____ of noisy birds wakes me up
every morning.

1 mark

14 There was a layer of _____ at the bottom of the jar.

1 mark

15 Flo's _____ new puppy nipped my fingers.

1 mark

16 The _____ to the throne is learning how to perform
royal duties.

1 mark

17 The _____ weightlifter won the champion's trophy.

1 mark

18 Nelson Mandela did a lot to stop _____ against
black people in South Africa.

1 mark

19 After a long holiday, I always enjoy the _____ of
home.

1 mark

20 The doctor gave me a _____ to the hospital when I
injured my wrist.

1 mark

Total marks .... /20   How am I doing? ☺ 😐 ☹

Listen carefully to the missing word and fill in the answer space.

1 The exhausted explorers were relieved when their

_____ came to an end.

1 mark

2 It is important not to exceed the _____ dose.

1 mark

3 There was a _____ figure walking in the fog.

1 mark

4 My mum bought an _____ Christmas tree.

1 mark

5 It is _____ hard to believe that we will be in
secondary school soon.

1 mark

6 Matt and Gem stirred the _____ until it melted.

1 mark

7 Mum and Dad were having a _____.

1 mark

8 The _____ leaders met to discuss ways to help
the homeless in our country.

1 mark

9 The two friends _____ with each other by post.

1 mark

10 We decided the good points about school _____
the bad points.

1 mark

11 The _____ in Zara's sketch was excellent.

1 mark

12 After a rather _____ journey, we arrived safely in the snowy mountains.

1 mark

13 If we are not _____ in how we use energy, we will have huge bills to pay.

1 mark

14 It was quite _____ that we met Maire as she was able to give us a lift home.

1 mark

15 At the summit of Mount Everest, the air is thin as there is less

_____.

1 mark

16 Our _____ told us our car needed a new battery.

1 mark

17 The _____ behaviour of Callum resulted in the whole class staying behind at lunchtime.

1 mark

18 At the _____ of his career, Alfred earned more money in a day than most people earned in a year.

1 mark

19 After our trip to the museum, we were asked to write

a _____ report.

1 mark

20 Although he can be quite _____, my brother is usually kind to me.

1 mark

Total marks .... /20   How am I doing? 😊 😐 😣

Notes

Acknowledgements

Every effort has been made to trace copyright holders and obtain their permission for the use of copyright material. The author and publisher will gladly receive information enabling them to rectify any error or omission in subsequent editions. All facts are correct at time of going to press.

Published by Collins
An imprint of HarperCollins*Publishers*
1 London Bridge Street,
London SE1 9GF

© HarperCollins*Publishers* Limited

ISBN 9780008201616

First published 2016

10 9 8 7 6 5 4 3 2 1

British Library Cataloguing in Publication Data.

A CIP record of this book is available from the British Library.

Commissioning Editor: Michelle l'Anson
Author: Shelley Welsh
Project Management and Editorial: Fiona Kyle and Katie Galloway
Cover Design: Sarah Duxbury and Paul Oates
Inside Concept Design: Paul Oates and Ian Wrigley
Text Design and Layout: Contentra Technologies
Production: Lyndsey Rogers
Printed and bound in China by RR Donnelley APS